Original title:
A Jungle in a Jar

Copyright © 2025 Creative Arts Management OÜ
All rights reserved.

Author: Thomas Sinclair
ISBN HARDBACK: 978-1-80581-848-9
ISBN PAPERBACK: 978-1-80581-375-0
ISBN EBOOK: 978-1-80581-848-9

Echoing Tranquility

In a world so small, critters dance,
A tiny frog hops in a chance.
A spider spins webs, a wondrous sight,
While ants march on, with all their might.

The goldfish swims in a silly twirl,
In bubbles they laugh, give a whirl.
An elephant's sneeze? Oh what a fuss!
In this glass land, there's joy for us.

The Dappled Light within Limitation

A parrot screeches in vibrant tones,
While lizards play hide and seek with stones.
The sun shines down on a mossy throne,
In a land where tall tales are often grown.

The beetles march with great intent,
On a leaf they find their main event.
A funny sight, they spin around,
In this small space, laughter is found.

Microcosm of the Wild

A rabbit twitches, ears perked high,
With broccoli trees, oh my, oh my!
The ants carry crumbs, a feast for the brave,
In this tiny realm, they misbehave.

The snail wears a shell, a house so neat,
While crickets chirp a buzzing beat.
The sun sets slowly, but they stay awake,
In this little world, they mime and shake.

Enigmas of the Enclosed

A mouse in a cap plays the flute,
Waltzing around in his tiny suit.
Funny beasts gather for tea,
Discussing great plans of wild jubilee.

The chameleon changes, oh what a show,
With colors so bright, they steal the show.
In their small kingdom, they laugh and tease,
Where each silly moment is sure to please.

Echoing Life in a Shard

In a glass box, critters prance,
Tiny feet in a wobbly dance.
Frogs wear hats made from a leaf,
While ants debate their next motif.

Lizards play hide and seek with ease,
Echoes bounce among the trees.
A snail sings out a slow, sweet tune,
Beneath the glow of a plastic moon.

Unspoken Voices of the Green

Within these walls, life softly shouts,
Sassy plants with leafy snouts.
Mice wear capes and plot their schemes,
Crafting dreams in sunlit beams.

Crickets chirp their silly rhymes,
Counting all the passing times.
A wandering bug drops a snack,
While worms groove to a disco track.

A Crystal Garden of Whimsy

A flower speaks in vivid hues,
Whispers secrets to the dews.
Bees do tap dance on the rim,
As fairies hum a jaunty hymn.

Clouds of fluff float on the breeze,
Tickling noses with such ease.
In a jar, such laughter swells,
Where curiosity compels.

Solitary Symphony of Growth

One lone sprout stands proud and tall,
In a world so small, it feels like all.
With a wink, it sways and bends,
To the rhythm only it transcends.

A caterpillar tries to improvise,
In a mini parade, it waves hi.
Each leaf dances to its own sweet tune,
While shadows play beneath the noon.

The Orchid's Confession

In a glass house, I plot and scheme,
With a fern as my partner in crime.
We dance at noon in the warm sunbeam,
While the window cleaner thinks we mime.

A cactus joins in with prickly flair,
He tells us jokes, but we never care.
He pokes fun at the daisies so fair,
They blush red, but we just laugh and stare.

Awakening in a Serenade

When morning sun spills through the glass,
The ferns all yawn, it's quite the scene.
The violets gossip, oh what a sass,
While I hum a tune with my morning bean.

A beetle waltzes, he's such a charmer,
With moves that would make a dancer weep.
We giggle and clap, oh what a farmer,
Growing laughter in soil so deep.

Green Sanctuary

Inside this vessel, a leafy crowd,
They throw wild parties, oh what a spree!
With tiny berries, and laughter loud,
Each sip of dew tastes like green tea.

The spider spins tales of grand escape,
We throw in snacks that smell like cheese.
In our snug corner, we're never late,
With leafy hats and jokes that tease.

In the Embrace of the Verdant

Snuggled close, the plants tell tales,
Of dancing roots and leafy cheer.
The light above and wind that hails,
Turns our tiny world into a sphere.

A ladybug struts, oh what a sight,
Claiming the throne of a mushroom top.
With banter bright in afternoon light,
We cheer him on, and the giggles won't stop.

Unseen Footfalls

Tiny creatures dance below,
In my glass home, they steal the show.
A snail with swag, a beetle's prance,
All my guests in a wild romance.

Their whispers echo in the night,
Footfalls soft, a funny sight.
Who knew my jar could host a ball?
With critters having quite a brawl?

Untamed Beauty Encapsulated

A fern that thinks it's queen of pride,
Waves its fronds, no need to hide.
Mossy carpets, lush and green,
In this small world, they're truly mean.

Tiny vines climb the glassy wall,
Wrestling roots, they have a ball.
The petals giggle, colors bright,
In their own fashion, they take flight.

The Stillness of Growth

In the quiet, sprouts arise,
Peeking gently, nature's surprise.
A leaf yawns wide, an early bloom,
Giggles echo in this cramped room.

A sprout challenges the wilted sage,
As if to say, 'I'm on the stage!'
A quiet riot, roots entwine,
In this glass world, it's all divine.

Trapped in Green Splendor

Here's a party, but I'm the host,
Each green guest, I love the most.
Caterpillars munch with glee,
What a sight; they dance for me!

In this splendor, all are free,
But who's the one that cannot flee?
Giggling leaves, they seem to plot,
While I sit—what a funny spot!

Secrets of Leafy Treasures

In a glass tower, green things sway,
Little critters dance and play.
A snail wears shades, oh what a sight,
In this tiny world, everything's right.

The moss claims fame, a velvet throne,
While ants give speeches, quite well-known.
A ladybug sings, with joy so pure,
In this cozy realm, mischief is the lure.

The sunbeam peeks, the shadows flee,
A parrot's gossip, who could it be?
Lizards wear shirts, that's the new trend,
Who knew nature could so much blend?

With laughter bright, this glassy view,
Unlikely pals, a motley crew.
Secrets whispered, stories unfold,
In leafy corners, where life is bold.

A Bottled Eden

In a bottle, bright and funny,
Bumblebees buzz, living sunny.
Red ants dance in a conga line,
While crickets play tunes so divine.

A cactus struts with a spiky hat,
While beetles chat about the latest spat.
A fern fluffs up, claiming it's a star,
In this chamber, they dream bizarre.

Worms throw a gala, up on the moss,
Sharing tales of how they toss.
A dragonfly twirls in a ballet grace,
Who knew this bottle could hold such space?

They plot and scheme, yet all in jest,
In their glass home, they're truly blessed.
With laughter echoing, their joy's divine,
A bottled Eden, oh how they shine!

Enigma in Transparent Quiet

In a crystal world, where giggles grow,
A chubby frog puts on a show.
With glasses perched, and a bowtie neat,
He croaks a tune with a jazzy beat.

Bugs in tuxedos attend the ball,
While ferns flutter, having a ball.
A grasshopper's joke gets all the laughs,
As vines weave tales of daring staffs.

In the stillness, whispers float,
About a lizard who dreams to gloat.
A tiny squirrel wants to play chess,
In this quiet plot, oh what a mess!

Windows sparkle with nature's cheer,
In their world, there's nothing to fear.
With secrets safe, they all abide,
In this echoing glass, where smiles reside.

Nature's Guardians Entombed

Tiny frogs in tiny hats,
Dance around like silly gats.
A tribe of bugs with jolly tunes,
Happily prancing 'neath plastic moons.

A beetle leads a conga line,
While crickets sip on fizzy brine.
A lizard struts with goofy flair,
Wishing for a wig, or maybe hair.

Shades of Serenity in Glass

In a bottle, fish float by,
Wearing scarves and all ask why.
With giddy swirls, the seaweed twirls,
As clowns in bubbles make their whirls.

The snails hold court, with regal grace,
But slip and slide—a race to chase!
A crab in shades—what a cool dude,
Playing tunes to lift the mood.

The Captured Wild

A grasshopper plans his escape,
With dreams of racing at top shape.
While moths throw shade, all in a jam,
Dancing round the cookie gram.

The ants have formed a marching band,
In tiny boots, they take a stand.
A squirrel knocks; it wants a try,
In cookie crumbs, the snacks run dry.

A Reverie of Roots

In a jar, the roots hold court,
They're scheming deep—a plant report.
With whispers soft, the dirt confides,
While little worms play on slides.

A thistle dreams of winning sprout,
With hopes of going all-out,
And when the light begins to fade,
The shadows dance, a grand parade.

Nature's Miniature Sanctuary

In a glass box, the crickets croon,
Tiny frogs dance beneath the moon.
A leaf serves as a cozy bed,
While ants march on with dreams in their head.

The world is small, but oh, so bright,
A ladybug dons her polka dot flight.
Bees buzzing close, though they can't roam far,
Just a sip of nectar from a candy jar.

Secrets in a Sealed World

Oh look! A snail, he's wearing a hat,
A spider's spinning tales, how about that?
With twigs and stones, the critters play,
In this tiny realm, they frolic all day.

A frog with dreams of a glittering stage,
While a worm reads poems from an old page.
Every leaf holds a secret and grin,
In this mini cunning realm, we dive right in!

Wild Echoes in Clear Enclosure

In a world of glass, the chatter is loud,
Bouncing and clattering, oh how they crowd!
A beetle wears shades, a real cool chap,
While a millipede struts his leggy claptrap.

The flowers nod to the bouncy beat,
As a tiny lizard rocks to the heat.
Here's a concert for those who may peek,
A raucous show, a wild freaky sneak!

Captured Canopy

A thimble's top, with treasures inside,
Grass blades and petals, all in a ride.
The moths joke with fireflies at dusk,
While the ants play tag among the musk.

A crumpled leaf is their perfect slide,
And shenanigans flourish, full of pride.
In this playful patch, they wiggle and wriggle,
A marvelous world, where laughter is giggle!

The Cozy Canopy

In a glassy chamber, critters creep,
Tiny frogs hop, while the fireflies leap.
Lizards lounge on branches of moss,
Who knew a spoon could hold such a gloss?

Ants march along like they're on a spree,
In this mini forest, all's wild and free.
A sip of juice makes a slimy snail,
Racing through leaves like a wacky whale!

Each twist and curl brings a new delight,
A gerbil's vacation is a comical sight.
Squirrels pop corn—oh what a show!
In this tiny realm, the antics just flow!

The skies are bright, though it's always night,
Nature's funhouse, all parties in sight.
A world in a bottle, to giggle and gawk,
Who knew the fun was just one small talk?

Nature's Enigma in a Vessel

Inside this globe, a mystery brews,
Tiny beasts plan mischief, wearing bright shoes.
A plump little hedgehog rolls in delight,
While ants play chess till the morning light.

Butterflies fashion their gowns in the breeze,
Counting the petals, they're sure to tease.
A parrot squawks lines from a very old flick,
In this glassy realm, time doesn't tick.

Grasshoppers host a raucous dance,
Creating a rhythm, they take their chance.
A peeking goldfish dons spectacles wide,
Admiring the chaos, he beams with pride!

With each twist, the plot thickens and flows,
Carnival chaos, oh how it grows.
Life in this bottle, such cheeky delight,
In nature's strange ways, we find our light!

Eclectic Green Haven

In a jar of wonders, the colors collide,
Crickets compose, each in their stride.
A monkey's wild laugh echoes through leaves,
As a snail plays hide and seek behind peas.

Bottled up chaos, what a delightful mess,
Sloths play checkers with speed they possess.
Chameleons change hues just for the thrill,
While beetles negotiate a dance on the hill.

Mice fashion capes from forgotten rags,
Swinging on vines made of old shopping bags.
Raccoons throw parties with snacks piled high,
In this odd habitat, we laugh till we cry!

With worms all around, as dancers they twist,
Making a ruckus, oh what a tryst!
Within this odd space, giggles abound,
In a world so fantastic, joy can be found!

Shadows of the Verdant World

Beneath the glass dome, mischief unfolds,
Tales of adventures, each creature beholds.
Crabs wear sunglasses—the fashion's sublime,
In a world that's aquatic, all things seem prime.

The vine tries to sneak into the soup pot,
While frogs giggle over a funny old plot.
A gopher in pigtails spins tales of yore,
As butterflies gather, they dance on the floor.

With whispers and chuckles, the gang is alive,
In the shadows of green, they manage to thrive.
A snail with a trumpet makes music so loud,
While a bear plays the drums and attracts a crowd!

So here in this habitat, laughter is king,
Nature's secrets tucked in—a crazy old fling.
With each little giggle, creates an embrace,
In this jar of shadows, we find our own space!

Nature's Bottled Whispers

In a glass world, plants do sway,
Where tiny creatures laugh and play.
A tree so small, it won't outgrow,
Yet dances high, with roots below.

Beetles strut with fancied flair,
Grasshoppers leap without a care.
Ants throw parties, munching crumbs,
While lizards pose and strike their thumbs.

The sun shines bright, but just for show,
In a tiny realm where breezes blow.
With every sip, the jungle sings,
Of buzzing bees and fluttering wings.

With a twist, the cap goes tight,
And all the fun is sealed at night.
But dreams of green will never cease,
In this small world, there's wild release.

A Flora's Tale

There once was a flower, shy and sweet,
With petals that knew no need for heat.
It whispered jokes to the air around,
While a little worm rolled on the ground.

"Why do leaves never get lost?" it cried,
"They know how to cling, and they've got pride!"
A rabbit chuckled from the ferny base,
As the flower giggled, "This is our place!"

Clouds looked down with a knowing glance,
As the plants below began to dance.
They twirled and spun in the glassy light,
While beetles cheered, "What a silly sight!"

So next time you water, take a peek,
At the whims of nature, so unique.
In this little home, laughter grows,
In hilarious tales that nobody knows.

Secrets Behind Clear Walls

Behind the glass, a world so bright,
Where fungi hide and bugs take flight.
A secret life in silence hums,
And mischief waits until night comes.

A snail with dreams of quick escape,
Plotting grand journeys, make no mistake.
While ladybugs strut in zany pairs,
Joking about their shiny wares.

Moss whispers secrets of fungi friends,
As they dance together, making amends.
The pebbles joke, "We sure are neat,
Getting stomped by every little feet!"

So peek inside at this view so lush,
Where chaos reigns in a gentle hush.
Each creature spins stories, full of cheer,
In this quaint land where fun draws near.

Boundless Creatures of Small Spaces

In tiny corners, critters thrive,
With vibrant adventures in their hive.
A spider spins tales of mirth,
While ants parade across the earth.

A bumblebee buzzes a secret song,
As crickets chirp, "Come join along!"
The mossy carpet holds a stage,
Where creatures gather to engage.

The fish in a bowl wear crowns of glee,
As they frolic in bubbles, wild and free.
"Splash and swirl!" they chant with glee,
Creating a party for all to see.

Each pop and fizz brings giggles near,
In this glass world, there's nothing to fear.
So shake your lid, and let them out,
For a raucous jam with laughs and shouts!

A Fragmented Forest

In a glass case, ferns do sway,
Tiny critters join the play.
Mossy rocks, a hamster's glee,
A party for ants, you see!

Mushrooms dance without a care,
The goldfish gives a baffled stare.
Lizards lounge, a sight so grand,
While the snail conducts a band!

Twitching roots, they start to lean,
A squirrel's scheme, a hidden bean.
Bamboo stalks forming a brawl,
In this jar, all seem so small!

The air is thick, a comic act,
Every leaf holds a goofy fact.
In this world, all's a jest,
Nature's stage, a laughing fest!

The Boxed Botanist's Dream

In my jar, a wild affair,
Cacti dancing everywhere.
Sunflowers grin, a cheerful lot,
While peas huddle in a plot.

Berry bushes full of sass,
Rabbits race, they're made of glass!
A mismatched crew, what a scene,
Even grasshoppers like to preen!

Roses brag with fragrant flair,
Petunias gossip, unaware.
Time to water, what a fuss,
Can't believe they're all this much!

Chasing crickets, with a hop,
Who will sing the funny top?
All contained, yet full of cheer,
In this dream, there's nothing here!

Urban Wilderness Coiled

Inside my glass, a wild escape,
A rubber snake, a funny shape!
Potted plants, they start to feign,
Pretend to sip from drops of rain.

A squirrel struts on tiny feet,
While turtles cheer from their front seat.
Whiskers twitch, the fish will leap,
Into my dreams, no time for sleep!

Frogs in bowties croak a tune,
Cacti skate like they're on a moon.
Lizards boast, their skills in style,
While daisies giggle all the while!

The windows shake, the laughter grows,
In this jar, mirth freely flows.
Urban dreams in vibrant threads,
Nature's party, full of spreads!

Whispers of the Enclosed Wild

In a bottle, creatures scheme,
Rats in hats, oh what a dream!
A parrot paints the walls in red,
While snails play a game instead!

The insects throw a masquerade,
Petals blush, their colors fade.
A butterfly with glee does flip,
A tiny taco on a trip!

The fern's a chef, and quite renowned,
Cookin' up fun without a sound.
With laughter echoing night and day,
In this world, they frolic and play!

So tap your foot to nature's beat,
In this jar, life feels so sweet.
A comic tale beneath the sun,
Enclosed delight, just having fun!

Fractured Forest in Fragments

Tiny trees in glass, all trimmed,
A twinkling world, where dreams are skimmed.
A lizard playing peekaboo,
In a mini-world of green and blue.

Frogs wear hats, they sit and stare,
Comically confused in their little lair.
Mice in suits argue for cheese,
In this odd space where nothing's quite at ease.

The rivers ran with soda pop,
Turtles flip-flopped and wouldn't stop.
From one side to the other they hopped,
In this fractured zone, all logic dropped.

Every critter sports a grin,
Each tiny adventure feels like a win.
In their glassy paradise so bizarre,
Life's a laugh beneath the jar.

Echoes of the Untamed

Whispers of leaves dance in a spin,
As critters plot their capers with a grin.
Rabbits juggling carrots in a row,
While birds tweet secrets no one should know.

Sloths have disco parties on a limb,
With tiny beats that don't quite fit the whim.
Surprised by all the ruckus below,
They join in the fun, bashful and slow.

A snail with shades oozes his charm,
While ants march in line, causing alarm.
In chaotic rhythm, they bust out a groove,
A jungle of giggles, eternally on the move.

Echoes of laughter bounce off the glass,
Creating a joy that is sure to amass.
Living wild, yet neat and contained,
In an untamed realm, humor is gained.

The Surrendered Wilderness

A parrot speaks in riddles and rhymes,
In this odd world, it's lost track of time.
Beneath the palm, a party unfolds,
With tales of cheeky mischief retold.

In this surrendered space they prance,
Squirrels in tutus lead the dance.
Chasing after jokes and a stray bumblebee,
They're wild yet contained in this oddity.

Ferrets in bow ties, oh what a sight,
Curiosity peeking with pure delight.
Each critter conspires more silliness,
In their glassy haven, they're free of stress.

Laughter erupts like a fizzy drink,
Reality's blurred, just stop and think.
In the wilderness that happily plays,
Humor's the heart of their curious ways.

Glassbound Greenery

Frogs in top hats and tails that twirl,
Secretly gossip of the nearby whirl.
Their laughter echoes, oh what a spree,
In glassbound greenery, wild and free.

Ants play chess on a leaf so wide,
Pondering moves as their thoughts collide.
The winners boast, the losers pout,
In this tiny world where fun's all about.

Butterflies have wings of disco lights,
Flitting about like dazzling sights.
They can't decide where the party's at,
So they host it all in their leafy habitat.

A jar so small, yet bursting with cheer,
Its inhabitants thrive without a fear.
With giggles and whimsy in every nook,
This glassy realm's a humorous book.

Tiny Kingdoms of Green

In a glass box, plants all aglow,
Tiny creatures put on a show.
Frogs in tuxedos, dancing on leaves,
Ants wearing hats, oh, what a tease!

Cacti are kings, they stand so tall,
While lizards in shorts have a ball.
Moss in the corner holds a grand feast,
Where snails sip tea, it's a quirky beast!

Bugs take selfies, the lights are bright,
Grasshoppers jump in sheer delight.
Life in this realm is quite absurd,
Every day's filled with funny word!

A miniature world, what a delight,
With laughter and joy, it's a silly sight.
Green and vibrant, it brings a cheer,
In our little realm, there's nothing to fear!

Captured Wilderness

In a jar so snug, wild things reside,
With tiny tigers that snugly hide.
Crickets play chess with a firefly flair,
While spiders spin webs of silky air.

A parakeet sings, though it never flew,
Dancing with moss—oh, what a view!
Rabbits wear glasses and read some lore,
A party in here, who could ask for more?

The leaves are green with a touch of gold,
Stories of mischief endlessly told.
In this confined, bustling estate,
Life feels like a comedy, isn't it great?

Captured wonders, all in a round,
From midnight parties to daylight sound.
In our dance hall, the laughter is grand,
In this tiny space, it's perfectly planned!

Secrets of the Glass Oasis

Behind glass walls, we see the fun,
With critters that dance, in the light of the sun.
Tropical myths, under a palm tree,
Where bugs recite poetry, oh, so free!

Vines twist and turn like a jolly vine,
While frogs sing duets, oh so divine.
Lizards with attitude flaunt their style,
In this miniature land, they go the extra mile.

Beetles in bow ties and ants that cater,
A gala awaits, it couldn't be greater!
Filled with charm and giggles galore,
In our glass oasis, who could want more?

Secrets unfold like petals so bright,
As the stars come to join in the night.
Each laughter echoes, each creature a star,
In our whimsical world, there's joy from afar!

Lush Dreams in Crystal Walls

Within crystal walls, verdant dreams thrive,
With tiny critters that happily strive.
A giraffe with spots drinks from a dew,
While butterflies gossip, sharing the view!

Cats on the prowl, oh so polite,
Preening and posing in the soft light.
Fleas crafting fashion, they strut with pride,
In this little kingdom, there's nowhere to hide.

Trees made of tinsel, breathtakingly bright,
Twilight fills the area with shimmer and light.
Gnats on parade, they twirl and they spin,
Every day brings new chaos and grin!

A world so wild, yet fit to hold,
The craziest tales, all waiting to unfold.
In our lush dreams, full of surprises,
The fun never ends, just endless rises!

Secrets of the Enclosed Canopy

In my glassy world, a creature sneezes,
A leaf takes flight, and my foot tickles,
Lizards do backflips, oh what a sight,
While ants play tag under moonlit nights.

A frog does yoga, strikes a pose,
With each stretch, the jar explodes!
Beetles wear suits, oh what a scene,
An insect party, both wild and keen.

Inside my vessel, the chaos grows,
A dance of petals, where no one knows,
Caterpillars whisper, secrets unfold,
Beneath leafy roofs, stories retold.

The air is thick with mischief and cheer,
Giggling crickets, the sounds I hear,
In this tiny realm, both weird and grand,
Life's a riddle, on a whim it spins sand.

Nature's Symphony in Solitude

Inside my glass dome, a whimsical tune,
The fireflies flicker, and dance like a loon,
Grasshoppers strum on an acorn guitar,
While spiders conduct from the edge of a jar.

A snail hums softly, with fingers so spry,
To the beat of the cricket, oh, how he'll fly!
Bees buzz together in a merry parade,
With a banner of pollen, their sweet serenade.

The lizards laugh, wearing hats made of leaf,
As mushrooms join in, sharing tales of grief,
Yet the laughter echoes, for all must agree,
In my tiny domain, we're all wild and free.

Open the lid for a moment or two,
And watch as they scatter, hilariously askew,
Nature's grand concert, a sight to behold,
In glassy confines, where fun never gets old.

Glistening Bottles of Green

Glistening bottles, full of delight,
In each tiny bubble, creatures take flight,
A hedgehog in goggles looks ready to dive,
With dreams of adventure, how could they survive?

The vines chuckle softly, tickling their friends,
While each droplet winks and only pretends,
A parrot in sequins, all dressed to impress,
While peppers do pirouettes to cheer the rest.

A grand masquerade under shimmering glow,
Where crickets spin tales of the winds that they know,
Dancing on marbles, the whole jar's aglow,
Oh, what a party in this vibrant show!

But close that lid quickly, don't let them escape,
For outside they'd find no more glittering cape,
Inside is their haven, their playground, their sheen,
In glistening bottles, they reign like a queen.

Echoes from the Shards

Amidst shattered shards, a world takes its stage,
With twinkle-lit spirits, how clever, how sage,
A squirrel in glasses, a feathered debate,
Discussing the best ways to make whiskers straight.

Beneath the cracked glass where sunlight will gleam,
Insects aim high – it's a glittery dream,
A parade of the weird, a comical sight,
As they wobble and shuffle, oh, what a delight!

The bottle is buzzing, a raucous affair,
With worms doing waltzes, without a care,
A lizard named Larry, sporting a crown,
"Long live the jar!" he declares with a frown.

Echoes of laughter, from the shards they make,
Their tiny adventures, no chance for a break,
In a world of mischief, they frolic about,
With each little laughter, they dance and shout!

Behind the Glass

Inside this glass, oh what a sight,
Tiny critters dance, full of delight.
A snail on a leaf, feeling quite grand,
He thinks he's the king of this miniature land.

A frog takes a leap with a comical flair,
While ants hold a meeting, a serious affair.
All watch a snail at an epic slow race,
Who will win? It's a test of pace!

A twig's their tower, a pebble's their throne,
In this tiny world, they're never alone.
Under a moss, a secret is spun,
Life in a jar? Oh what fun!

Yet, when I peek, they all freeze, it's true,
"Act natural!" they squeak; they've no clue.
Behind the glass, their ruckus is clear,
What a wild show when no humans are near!

Mysteries of the Leafed Realm

In the shade of a leaf, a caterpillar lies,
Whispering tales to the newly arrived flies.
"Life's a buffet, just munch and don't care,
But watch out for danger—like my uncle the bear!"

A beetle rolls treasure, a crumb from my lunch,
While a ladybug giggles, "Ha! What a bunch!"
The vibrant green looks like an intricate maze,
Filled with odd characters, a jungle of plays.

And then there's that lizard who thinks he's so sly,
Riding on leaves as the butterflies fly.
He jumps out in jest, doing a flip,
Causing a ruckus, a stumblin' trip!

In this tiny kingdom, full of quirks and glee,
Every leaf has its own hidden story, you see.
Life's full of mischief when you're small and zany,
In this green empire, it's all just so grainy!

The Keystone of Nature

Beneath the glass dome, life teems and jives,
With each grass blade, countless humor arrives.
A glob of a jelly, oh what a scene,
It's the party of life, in a world so serene.

A cricket recites while the roaches applaud,
A drama unfolds in the space they all trod.
In the sand at the bottom, a turtle has dreams,
Of grander adventures beyond glassy beams.

The weeds have their wisdom; they gossip all day,
In a patch of fine soil, they always find play.
A game of hide-and-seek, who will invite?
The nuggets of laughter that fill up the night!

In a jar so confined, the chaos expands,
Nature's comedians craft wild, funny plans.
It's a ticket to joy, and I'm front row and clear,
In this zany habitat, I laugh with cheer!

Heartbeats in a Terrarium

In this glass booth, a heartbeat's gone wild,
Where a worm is a dancer, nature's own child.
The grass shakes and shimmers with secrets galore,
As lizards play tag, then go back for more.

A quick little mouse plays hide from a ghost,
Only to find he's the one they all roast.
"I'm not that scary!" he squeaks in a squeal,
Yet the bugs burst with laughter, it's a comedic reel.

A dance of the leaves as the wind softly sighs,
Each twig and each leaf forms a surprise.
Under the glass, where laughter's the goal,
Life in a jar has its very own soul.

From beetles to bunnies, they all make a fuss,
Together they giggle; they're part of the bus.
So here's to their heartbeats, their giggles and charms,
In this tiny domain, it's joy that warms!

The Glassy Microbiome

Inside my glass abode, things giggle and sway,
Tiny critters dance, making night feel like day.
Frogs on a lily pad, wearing hats of bright blue,
They croak out their tunes, creating quite the view.

Ants march in line, with snacks on display,
Feasting on crumbs that I'd thrown away.
They host their grand parties on the kitchen floor,
While I sip my tea, laughing at their roar.

A snail wearing glasses, slows down the fun,
Reading the news, oh what tales he spun!
Bubbles rise high, like champagne in cheer,
In this lively world, I hold so dear.

So here in this jar, we all get along,
A raucous community, a merry throng.
Life in the glass, a whimsical show,
In this miniature realm, joy continues to grow.

Enclosed Ecstasy

Within these clear walls, the laughter runs free,
Animals prance about, filled with glee.
A monkey swings high, hanging on for dear life,
While a turtle plays poker, avoiding the strife.

The parrot gabs gossip, with every squawk,
While down by the water, the goldfish just talk.
They share all their secrets, in bubbles they form,
Creating a dialogue, clever and warm.

Cockroaches throw parties, with cupcakes and pie,
While the garden they've grown makes me sigh and comply.
Mice dance on the table, wearing shoes made of cheese,
In this happy habitat, my worries just freeze.

So here in this chamber, let all spirits soar,
Together we chuckle, forever explore.
With absurdity reigning, life takes on a cheer,
In this comical kingdom, nothing's unclear.

A Tangle of Tranquility

Inside my clear kingdom, chaos seems right,
A ferret on stilts, such a comical sight!
The flowers are chatting, like gossiping pals,
As vines weave together, turning lattes to jowls.

A tiny giraffe peeks, stretching tall for a view,
While a hamster critiques, with a beret, it's true!
Rabbits hold matches, to light up the scene,
Creating a carnival, of colors so keen.

A snail in a tux, serves cheese on a tray,
While frogs on a trampoline bounce all the day.
Whimsical moments, like rainbows they twirl,
In this little habitat, my imagination swirls.

Chasing the critters, I laugh as they flee,
In this tangled-up world, it's pure harmony.
With friends from the wild, under glass we thrive,
In this hub of hilarity, we feel so alive!

Wilderness Within Walls

Beneath my clear cover, wild antics unfurl,
A raccoon in pajamas starts to spin and twirl.
The beetles, they jive, with moves that amaze,
While crickets keep time, in a musical blaze.

Chameleons chuckle, changing hues in a flair,
Laughing at squirrels, who think they can share.
The plants start to giggle, with each gentle sway,
As they watch the antics unfold day by day.

A hedgehog in shades, sipping juice from a straw,
Claims he's the king, but let's not give a paw!
Dancing through petals, everyone bops,
In this cramped wilderness, the laughter just pops.

With laughter encrypted in every single crack,
The creatures unite, no one ever looks back.
In this enclosed wonder, absurdity reigns,
As my jar full of crazy, keeps joy in the chains.

The Nature Within

In a tiny world, bugs dance around,
Sipping dew drops, not a sound.
Frogs in hats play poker all night,
While ants in suits take flight!

The grass is this high, the trees are so small,
A great big bumblebee barely can crawl.
Fireflies flash like stars in a play,
Who knew paradise could fit on display?

Mice are munching on cake made of clay,
While flowers gossip about the day.
A snail in a shell takes a ride on a leaf,
Whispering tales of vegetable grief.

Every leaf laughs with a tickle of breeze,
Critters bobbing like they're playing freeze.
In this quirky place, all seems quite fun,
In the laughter of nature, there's never a run.

A Microcosm's Song

In a bottle of glass, there's quite a scene,
Dancing bugs wearing shoes that are green.
Giggling weeds tickle a teddy bear,
As bumblebees buzz through the fragrant air.

A raccoon with a monocle sips herbal tea,
While ladybugs hold a jamboree.
Chirping critters play the kazoo,
Oh what a concert! A riotous view!

Tiny elephants in the flower patch sway,
Hopping about like they're in a ballet.
Mice in pajamas stargaze at night,
Guessing the shapes of clouds in moonlight.

Gnome on a trampoline, what a great sight,
Jumping so high, he's defying all height.
The laughter erupts, you can't help but smile,
In this small realm, let's stay for a while.

Vines of Glass

In a world of glass, vines twist and twirl,
Snakes in bow ties cause quite a whirl.
Flickering fireflies wear their best shoes,
In this comical land, who could refuse?

A parrot with lashes, painted and bright,
Mocks the sun as it shines in delight.
Laughter and cheer leap like frogs on a street,
In this jar society, all is a treat.

Spiders weave webs made of candy and dreams,
While worms spin around on their jellybean beams.
A dance off erupts, with all critters in line,
Each taking turns, saying, "That move's divine!"

Ponds of gelatin wiggle and bob,
With frogs in tuxedos that shimmy and sob.
In the wackiest place, life's true colors show,
In this slippery paradise, laughter will grow!

The Enchanted Terrarium

Inside a glass dome, all the critters play,
Wearing tiny hats, they brighten the day.
A turtle in shades slides down a slide,
Giggles erupt as they swiftly glide.

Squirrels spill acorns, clink them like wine,
While mushrooms around them serve dinner divine.
Their fine little banquet, oh what a spread,
Each dish a creation that no one would dread.

A fairy on stilts juggles with style,
As frogs all croak out, "Let's stay for a while!"
A raucous parade, with beetles on drums,
Join in the fun, as everyone hums.

The warmth of the lights on the green little leaves,
Fills this small world with magical eves.
In this land of delight, the fun never ends,
In the realm of the tiny, all are good friends!

Alive Beneath the Surface

In the glass, a kerfuffle sways,
Tiny critters dance in a fray.
With a splash and a dash, they swirl and glide,
Beneath the lid, their secrets hide.

Silly frogs with their grand leaps,
Darting fish jump like they're in heaps.
Each bubble that pops makes a giggle sound,
In this tiny space, joy abounds!

A sleepy snail puts up his pace,
While a darting bug joins the race.
A world of uproar in a quart-sized land,
With raucous laughter at their command!

In their bustling kingdom of greens and blue,
Life unfolds in all that they do.
With the twist of a cap, adventure stirs,
In this merry realm, madness blurs!

Tamed Wilderness

An ant parade marches on the glass,
Each one hurries, none let time pass.
A wiggly worm does a comical dance,
While a hopeful bug hopes for a chance.

With careful hands, I toast this show,
Tamed little beasts, put on a glow.
A twig becomes a throne for the queen,
In this small wild, it's quite the scene!

Jumping jacks from a daring shard,
With every twist, this place is charred.
A riotous chaos, all in good fun,
In this glass mess, there's room for everyone!

The plants sway disco, as if in a trance,
While critters hold an impromptu dance.
Who knew such life could fit inside?
In my tiny jungle, I take great pride!

The Green Sanctuary of Stillness

In a jar of glass, a party brews,
With leaves that rustle and tiny snooze.
A sleepy lizard, eyes half-closed,
Pretends he's tough but merely dozed!

The quiet hum of bugs in flight,
A snail slips by in slow delight.
With every wiggle, and every squirm,
Nature's chaos makes my heart warm.

A bit of moss clings to the side,
Where shy little critters sometimes hide.
With a wiggle and giggle, they play peek-a-boo,
In this stillness, it feels brand new!

Fronds wave like hands, giving a cheer,
For the footloose critters, oh so dear.
Here in this sanctuary, laughter does swell,
A glassy realm, a wonderful spell!

A World Untangled

In a sphere of glass, a ruckus breaks,
With wriggling wonders and joyful quakes.
A tangled mess of roots and weeds,
Where each little critter never concedes.

An eager fish gives a silly flip,
While a toad sings a comical trip.
The moss is a playground, the leaves all cheer,
As friendly encounters unfold ever near.

A parade of ants brings a silly sight,
As they form a line with sheer delight.
Each tiny creature, in vibrant shades,
Creates a dance that never fades.

With laughter bubbling, my heart takes wing,
In every corner, there's joy to cling.
A world of merriment, so brightly strung,
In this glassy realm, we are forever young!

The Window to Wonder

Behind the glass, a wriggle,
A snail in a dance, oh so sly.
Beetles wear hats, they giggle,
As leaves flap their wings with a sigh.

A chameleon's sly little wink,
Plays hide and seek, with such flair.
As I pour a drink, I think,
Will the ants join in for a pair?

The world's so small, yet so grand,
With crickets that strum on the side.
A tiny parade in the sand,
Sipping sunshine, enjoying the ride.

In this nook of glee, so sweet,
Grasshoppers bounce like each cheer.
A carnival tucked by my feet,
Nature's antics always near.

Enclosed Dreams of Earth

Inside this glass, a vibrant spree,
Where daisies spin tales of delight.
A rabbit hops, so wild and free,
Chasing shadows in morning light.

Mice in tuxedos, ever so neat,
Tap dance on petals, what a show!
Caterpillars join, not to be beat,
Belly laughs shared in a glow.

Frogs wear crowns, the rulers fair,
Holding court on a lily pad throne.
While ants weave tales in the air,
Discussing mysteries not yet known.

This realm, a merry little jest,
With every twig, a laugh will bloom.
In tiny worlds, we're all guests,
Where joy and silliness make room.

The Echoing Heart of the Forest

In my vessel, wonders twirl,
Frogs wear crowns and strum sweet tunes.
Beetles play maracas, give a whirl,
As shadows dance beneath the moons.

A tiny fox with a sly little grin,
Taps a rhythm on a twig.
While fireflies join the din,
Lighting up the night, so big.

Crickets hum, a symphony free,
Braiding dreams with laughter too.
In each corner, wild whimsy, you see,
Leaves whisper secrets, just for you.

This merry maze, a crafty cheer,
Where every twist brings laughter's glow.
Join the fun, abandon your fear,
In this forest, let your spirit grow.

Petite Nature's Anthology

In this glass, a story unfolds,
With ants wearing bikes and a grin.
A butterfly's laughter, bright and bold,
As giggles and guffaws begin.

Snails huddle close for a game of chess,
While mushrooms speak of days gone by.
Underneath, roots laugh, no less,
Tickling toes as they jovially sigh.

Ladybugs twirl in a lively dance,
As the breeze carries tales so sweet.
In this small world, take a chance,
Joy blooms where magic and mischief meet.

So open the lid, let them all out,
Watch as they prance in a cup of cheer.
With every stumble and happy shout,
Nature's fun make life so dear.

Nurtured Chaos

In a glassy space, plants twist and twine,
Squirrels dance with glee, oh how they shine!
Frogs wear hats, they're quite the sight,
Chasing fireflies, they giggle with delight.

A cat dips a paw, gives it a try,
The critters all ponder, should they comply?
One tadpole slips, shouts, "It's a splash!"
As bamboo grows straight, it's quite the bash!

Rabbits hop in, bringing their stew,
Carrots for all, it's quite the zoo!
A parrot squawks jokes, what a silly tease,
While the fish all play cards, oh such a breeze!

In this little haven, laughter wins,
Who knew chaos thrived in such tiny bins?
With each wriggly wiggle and cheerful sound,
Life dances in jars, joyfully unbound.

Roots in a Receptacle

Tiny terrariums bustling with cheer,
Gossiping roots, lend me your ear!
Leprechauns tap-dance on snappy moss,
While ants wear tiny shoes, what a gloss!

In every nook, there's a comical scene,
Snakes curled around rocks, playing 'who's mean?'
Mice holding meetings, plotting a heist,
For crumbs of cheese, oh isn't that nice?

A wobbly turtle in a top hat prances,
He claims he's a prince, join in the dances!
While hedgehogs play poker with glee in the sun,
A snail throws confetti, aren't they just fun?

In closed-up spaces, where mischief brews,
A ruckus is forged, tight in their views.
As roots intertwine, they giggle and sway,
In this quirky life, it's forever play!

Tiny Kingdom of Verdure

A kingdom of green, sprouting within,
Lizards in crowns, where to begin?
Caterpillars scurry, ooh what a show,
Painting in colors, where giggles do flow.

In a pebble's shade, the crickets do cheer,
Playing their fiddles, oh do you hear?
While wise owls grumble, wrapped in debate,
About who's the fastest, what a great fate!

Feathers unfurl on squirrels in line,
A fashion parade, oh isn't it fine?
Ants march with pomp, in their little brigade,
Planning a feast for a wild charade!

A tiny domain filled with laughter and jest,
Turning each moment into a fest.
Where lush leaves cradle safe little dreams,
In this miniature world, all is not as it seems!

Enclosed Eden

In a pot of mischief, greenery thrives,
Puffballs of dandelions, oh how it strives!
Chickens wear glasses, reading the news,
Jabbering babbles, it's all just to amuse.

Napping between blooms, the ladybugs yawn,
Bouncing on petals, from dusk until dawn.
There's a fish in a bowl, with a lovely bow tie,
Sipping on roots, watching clouds go by.

Mice host a concert with spoons for a band,
Rabbits in tuxedos play tunes that are grand.
The soil is a stage, and the sun is the light,
Each day is a party, filled with delight!

With laughter as music, the leaves softly sway,
In this enclosed Eden, there's always a way.
For amidst the chaos, the fun always stays,
In this happy jar, where whimsy obeys!

Lush Labyrinth of Enchantment

In a jar so small and bright,
A jungle dances, what a sight!
The ants wear capes of leafy green,
And squirrels pirouette, so keen.

Monkey shines with mischief bold,
A tiny tiger, tales retold.
Each leaf a tale, each twig a joke,
In this jar, giggles provoked.

The spider spins a web of glee,
A jungle party, join the spree!
Fireflies waltz with open wings,
Who knew a jar could hold such things?

But watch your step, don't bump the lid,
Or this wild fun will surely skid.
A jar of joy, a wild charade,
In this small world, memories made.

Clarity of the Unfurling

Peering in this glassy realm,
Where rubber ducks take at the helm.
Giraffes eat snacks from jars of jam,
With giggles that go BAM! BAM! BAM!

A roly-poly rolls on by,
With patterns bright, oh my, oh my!
Each creature wears a silly hat,
While a pig thinks it's a diplomat.

There's bubbles bursting, popping cheer,
In this jar, there's no room for fear.
A festival of fun, oh what a show,
Who'd guess a jar could steal the glow?

So take a peek, let laughter bloom,
In every corner of this room.
With a twist and a turn, it's all absurd,
Welcome to the jokes unheard!

A World in Suspension

Bouncing in a bottle snug,
A bear hugs a teeny rug.
Marshmallow trees sway to the beat,
While critters jiggle in their seat.

A tap dancer on a stone so round,
The fastest snail can still astound.
In this space, they all convene,
To share a joke that's never seen.

Buglehorns and bubble tunes,
Silly songs under silver moons.
Each twist reveals a laugh or two,
In this space small, joy rings true.

But if you shake it, oh what fun,
The entire forest starts to run!
A glance inside might show a cheer,
In this microcosm, laughter near.

Flora's Forgotten Realm

In patches bright of purple bloom,
A gnome rides on a vacuum broom.
Each petal struts in silly ways,
Fashion shows for leafy fays.

A frog with shades on takes a leap,
While sleeping bugs all snore in heaps.
This patch of green has no dull stare,
It's tangled laughter everywhere.

The bees debate on who's the best,
While sipping nectar at a fest.
In this small nook of uproar joy,
Even daisies find time to annoy.

So if you peek, do so with care,
For laughter reigns in fragrant air.
In this forgotten, vibrant place,
Fun and whimsy weave with grace.

Whispers from the Verdant Depths

In a tiny realm where ferns converse,
The crickets wear their best attire.
A snail claims it has found a path,
While ants throw parties by the fire.

A beetle boasts of strange delights,
While shadows dance on mossy ground.
The whispers rise in chatter light,
In this green world where fun abounds.

Rustle of Leafy Spirits

Beneath the glass, where squirrels scheme,
The grasshoppers play hide and seek.
A dandelion insists it's queen,
And giggles at the winds that peek.

The twig men march in dandy rows,
While mushrooms host a tea for two.
Unseen mischief in every pose,
In leafy worlds, the laughter grew.

Glassy Edges of Eden

In crystal pockets, fun takes flight,
A hummingbird turns to a clown.
With every sip of morning light,
The sunbeams wear their golden crown.

The spiders weave a circus net,
And lizards stretch in comical ways.
What joys await, no need to fret,
In this small world of jolly plays.

Reflections of the Unseen

Look closer, friends, don't miss the fun,
Where shadows dance with silly grace.
A capybara just might run,
In high-top shoes, at a jolly pace.

With winks exchanged 'neath leafy veils,
The turtles might just start a band.
Their cheerful tunes float like soft sails,
In this glass realm of wonderland.

Symphony of Petals and Soil

In a tiny world, plants sway,
Like they just found a disco to play.
Earthworms groove to a bass line loud,
While ants form a marching crowd.

A beetle in shades, striking a pose,
Jumps on a leaf, as the fun grows.
Caterpillars dance, so bright and spry,
While butterflies laugh, flapping up high.

But watch out for the cheeky snail,
Who spins on a twig like it's a grand rail.
In this glassy realm, it's hard to believe,
That such silly antics can sprout and weave.

When twilight comes, the glowworms flash,
Creating a show, oh what a splash!
So grab your popcorn, find your seat,
For this show in a jar can't be beat!

Reflections of the Untamed

Tiny frogs croak their serenade,
While the restless vines begin to cascade.
A spider wears a glittery crown,
On its silky web, it won't drown.

Lizards chuckle, tails in a twist,
Playing tag with the morning mist.
A cricket with a top hat hops,
As a whispering breeze gently stops.

The pebbles nod with every pun,
As if they're all part of this fun run.
In this little world, such chaos reigns,
Where each little critter has wild refrains.

As night covers all in a silky veil,
The fireflies start their twinkling trail.
Nature's laughter in this glass space,
Bringing smiles, a real happy place!

Glassbound Flora

Through the glass, plants giggle and sway,
Debating on who leads the dance today.
Moss kicks back, feeling quite grand,
While ferns do the cha-cha, oh isn't it grand?

A thimble of rain serves as the stage,
For ants in tuxedos, a true rampage.
They twirl and dip, each move a surprise,
Wearing tiny top hats, oh my, oh my!

Petals shout, 'Let's have a ball!'
While dewdrops bounce, not afraid to fall.
Brightness spills out in a merry way,
In this quirky life, come join the play!

As moonlight peeks through the glass dome,
Frogs reclaim their royal throne.
In this spectacle so lively and bright,
Joy blooms eternal under the moonlight!

Bottled Tropics

In a bottle where laughter flows,
A parrot yells, 'Look at my clothes!'
A hippo in shades splashes around,
While a pufferfish wears a glittery crown.

Palm trees party with fruit cocktails,
While the banana leaves send funny tales.
The sunflowers giggle with every sway,
As shadows dance in a jazzy play.

The sandy floor hosts tiny shoes,
From antics bright as the tropical blues.
Turtles race in their slow-motion way,
With laughter echoing, come what may.

As night falls, the stars RSVP,
Cocooned in cheer, oh can't you see?
This bottled paradise sings so clear,
Inviting all with a joyous cheer!

Tangled Tendrils of Life

In a glass prison, roots twist tight,
A fern's rebellion, a leafy fight.
Lizards play tag, slip through the green,
Who knew such chaos could fit in between?

Moss on the rocks, a soft, fuzzy bed,
A snail takes a cruise, the slowest of tread.
Dancing dust mites take part in the fun,
While ants throw a party; they're never outdone!

A beetle, a dancer, spins with glee,
While spiders gossip, sipping on dew tea.
Tiny birds chirp in an accidental tune,
Crickets join in, to the rhythm of noon.

Every flip and flap brings laughter so bright,
In this little world, everything feels right.
Caught in a bottle, yet wild as can be,
Life's tangled tendrils, just wait and see!

Vibrant Whispers Encased

Whispers of laughter float through the air,
As gnats breakdance without a care.
A chubby little frog plays the jester's role,
Making a splash, a truly bold soul.

Petals interact with a light-hearted cheer,
While a sly beetle sneaks up near.
The sun sets inside, a golden delight,
Each shadow and shimmer a comic sight.

A curious worm tries to wiggle and squirm,
But finds glass boundaries far too firm.
With a tiny sigh, he recalls his home,
Where he could frolic, and freely roam.

Bubbles arise like laughter in flight,
Dancing and glimmering, what a delight!
This wild little world in a case so bright,
Where whispers and giggles take endless flight!

Green Haven within Glass

Inside a vessel, green dreams do thrive,
An ant parade marches, oh so alive!
Painted petals flutter, a colorful crew,
In this glass kingdom, chaos ensues.

Gnomes from the garden come out to play,
Planning mischief by night and by day.
A squirrel peeks in, curious and spry,
"Is that a fruit party?" he wonders, oh my!

A fish in a bowl thinks he's king of the scene,
While mossy companions are acting quite keen.
They share silly secrets and giggle in glee,
In this tiny habitat, the wild runs free!

Who needs the wild when you have all this?
A crazy collection of critters to kiss.
Each laugh that erupts, each joyful little zing,
In this green haven, life's a funny thing!

The Wild Within Borders

In a glass enclosure, the wild comes alive,
Giggling branches and vines all connive.
A dance floor of leaves, they shimmy and sway,
While ants do the conga, hip-hip-hooray!

A parrot on pause with a quirk in his glint,
Practices jokes in a bright, feathery tint.
The grasshoppers groove in their leafy attire,
With each little leap, they lift spirits higher.

A turtle who thinks he's a speed demon too,
Races the snails; oh, what a view!
As sunlight spills in, creating delight,
This bounded wildness thrives day and night.

With each little chuckle, a memory stays,
Of laughter and joy in these glassy displays.
In borders defined, the wild finds a way,
To tickle our senses and brighten our day!

Glistening Leaves in Solitude

Tiny leaves in a glass dome,
Whisper secrets, away from home.
A party of ants, they waltz and sway,
Claiming the floor, in their own little way.

Mossy carpets, plush and bright,
Dancing shadows in the light.
Laughter bubbles from within,
As raindrops tap, let the fun begin!

Feisty frogs join the lively spree,
Croaking tunes, as bold as can be.
A snail slips by, with style and grace,
In this wild world, there's no time to waste!

But wait! What's that? A curious fly,
Buzzing around, oh my, oh my!
It's a banquet for all, with no time to lose,
In this glassy realm, they simply refuse!

The Dreamscape Encased

Wiggly worms in a soil swirl,
Hosting a dance, give it a twirl.
A beetle brings chips, for a gourmet feast,
Who knew oh-so-small could become a beast?

A tiny parrot mimics with glee,
Imitating the cat, quite clever you see!
The garden grows great under moon's soft gaze,
In their cozy cradle, they'll bask for days.

Unicorns made from glittering clay,
Float through the air, with nothing to say.
Wobbling cacti tell jokes on the side,
As they poke at laughter, the fun won't hide!

In a world so small, joy's on parade,
Every creature joins in the charade.
With happiness bottled in this quirky space,
The essence of life, in a glassy embrace!

Ferns in a World of Glass

Ferns stretch high in the sunshine's warm glow,
Waving to passing bugs, putting on a show.
A lizard laughs, he's the king of this spot,
In his glassy kingdom, he can't be forgot.

Strawberries sprout with a mischievous grin,
Chasing a ladybug, ready to spin!
Tiny adventures hidden beneath,
In this verdant paradise, there's always some heft.

Shimmering dewdrops, like diamonds they rest,
Naughty little critters, never at rest.
Exploring the foliage, they giggle and leap,
In this glassy domain, no time for sleep!

A mouse in a tux, tiptoes on a leaf,
Winks at a spider, who's busy, no grief.
With laughter encased, life's joy multiplies,
In this vivid palace, where fun never dies!

Life's Enclave

Glittering pebbles, a whimsical maze,
Squiggly roots, in a playful daze.
The caterpillar rides a bubble's embrace,
Floating and giggling, what a silly race!

A snail in a hurry, well maybe not quite,
Tickled by grass, enjoying the light.
The petals cheer on, as if on a stage,
In this tiny world, they're all of one age.

Funky ferns like dancers in a trance,
Join in the party, they twist and prance.
A dance-off begins, oh what a delight,
In the jar of laughs, everything's bright!

When shadows stretch long, they bask in delight,
The fireflies come out to light up the night.
In this merry enclave where giggles collide,
Life's sweeter than candy, a joyous ride!

www.ingramcontent.com/pod-product-compliance
Lightning Source LLC
Chambersburg PA
CBHW050308120526
44590CB00016B/2542